This book is dedicated to
Dawn D., Donna M., and Sue A.

You ladies lived out your faith with strength and grace.
You taught me how to walk with Jesus every day of my life.

Scripture quotations taken from The Holy Bible, New International Version®, NIV®.
Copyright © 1973, 1978, 1984, 2011 by Biblica, Inc. Used with permission of
Zondervan. All rights reserved worldwide. www.zondervan.com.
Scripture quotations taken from the (NASB®) New American Standard Bible®,
Copyright © 1960, 1971, 1977, 1995, 2020 by The Lockman Foundation. Used by
permission. All rights reserved. lockman.org
Scripture quotations marked MSG are taken from The Message, copyright © 1993,
2002, 2018 by Eugene H. Peterson. Used by permission of NavPress. All rights
reserved. Represented by Tyndale House Publishers.
Scripture quotations marked CSB have been taken from the Christian Standard Bible®,
Copyright © 2017 by Holman Bible Publishers. Used by permission. Christian Standard
Bible® and CSB® are federally registered trademarks of Holman Bible Publishers.
Scripture quotations marked TPT are from The Passion Translation®. Copyright ©
2017, 2018, 2020 by Passion & Fire Ministries, Inc. Used by permission. All rights
reserved. ThePassionTranslation.com.
Scripture quotations marked (NLT) are taken from the Holy Bible, New Living
Translation, copyright ©1996, 2004, 2015 by Tyndale House Foundation. Used by
permission of Tyndale House Publishers, Carol Stream, Illinois 60188. All rights reserved.

ISBN - 978-1-952840-91-3

UNITED HOUSE Publishing Clarkston, Michigan
info@unitedhousepublishing.com www.unitedhousepublishing.com

Photography: Jessica Hutchmaker
Interior layout: Talitha McGuinness; talitha@unitedhousepublishing.com

Printed in the United States of America 2026 - First Edition

SPECIAL SALES
Most UNITED HOUSE books are available at special quantity discounts when
purchased in bulk by corporations, organizations, and special interest groups. For more
information, please email orders@unitedhousepublishing.com.

Endoresements

"I've had the joy of serving alongside Shannon in ministry and seeing her heart for helping women encounter Jesus in a real and life-changing way. She lives what she writes and has a gift for making Scripture come alive. Journey to the Cross will lead you into a deeper, more intimate walk with Jesus and, no matter what you're facing, continually point your heart back to Him."
— *Dianne Wyper, Author & Co-Founder of the Armor Up Women Community*

"For every woman who has a full plate, Journey to the Cross meets you right where you are—offering bite-sized devotions that refresh the soul. Each page invites you to pause, hear God's voice, and find joy again in your walk with Jesus."
— *Amber Olafsson, Founder of The Light Conference,*
Author of Armor Up, Owner of United House Publishing

Table of Contents

My Prayer for You

*But the Counselor, the Holy Spirit,
whom the Father will send in my name,
will teach you all things and
remind you of everything I have told you.*
John 14:26 (CSB)

*When the Counselor comes,
the one I will send to you from the Father —
the Spirit of truth who proceeds from the Father—
He will testify about me.
You also will testify, because
you have been with me from the beginning.*
John 15:26-27 (CSB)

*Dear Jesus,
Thank you that when You went to Heaven, You left the Holy Spirit for me. I want to
be teachable to all He has for me. May I be open to His voice to remember all You
have taught me. I give You this journey You took me on and ask that You bring it
to life for other women. I don't want this only for myself, but so that other women
may also see the freedom you offer–freedom that comes from being in a personal
walk with You. Use my journey to help women see their own journey–one that
draws them closer to You. A journey that encourages them to share with others all
that You are doing in their lives. A journey that doesn't end at the cross, but lives
on for all of our days. In Your name I pray…Amen.*

Introduction

Hello, my friend. I am so glad that you picked up this devotional. Let me start by telling you that *Journey to the Cross* is not about me, Shannon. It is about **YOU** and **YOUR** walk with Jesus. Hebrews 4:12 tells us that "God's word is alive and active." Every time you open your Bible, God wants to speak to you. He wants to use His word to draw you into a deeper relationship with Him. Whether you have read the Bible every day for years or this is your first time, God has something special planned for you as you take this journey.

Have you ever asked yourself how Jesus' time on earth relates to your life in the twenty-first century? Well, you are not alone. You see…that was me. I was doing my daily devotions, but not really taking God's word and applying it to my life. When I truly embraced God's Word being alive and active, I realized how much He wanted to teach me. I began to understand how much He wanted me to learn from His ministry on earth, His death on the cross, and His resurrection.

Journey to the Cross is **YOUR** personal walk with Jesus. Yes. . .I will use my walk with Him to share how He spoke to me, but then I will challenge you to look at your own life. That's what makes this devotional "alive and active." Each chapter has reflection questions for you to sit and reflect on what Jesus is saying to you. The scripture references are included so that you can dive into your Bible and read the accounts for yourself.

I encourage you to take your time as you read through this devotional. As a woman with a busy life, I have learned to break down any devotional or Bible study into smaller sections. This helped me feel less overwhelmed with the length. When I do this, I am able to truly hear what God is saying to me.

Here is a suggested process to help you through this journey:

> Day 1: Read the devotional - pray and ask Jesus how He is speaking to you;
>
> Day 2-4: Read the encounter with Jesus from your own bible - pray and ask Jesus how He is speaking to you;
>
> Day 5-7: Read the Reflection Question and ask Jesus to reveal how He wants you to respond.

My sister, I know this journey may be tough. If you are like me, you will be doing some searching and not like what you see. I am praying for you as you transform into the woman God has called you to be, a beautiful daughter of the King, who will walk in victory.

Let the Journey begin!

Chapter 1
What is My Purpose?

Jesus' ministry on earth was short, only three years. Those years were filled with so many teachings and miracles, it is overwhelming to know where to start. I asked God where He wanted our journey to start, and He led me to John the Baptist. He was Jesus' cousin. I like to imagine that they grew up together and played as best buddies. Scripture tells us that John was a little odd. He dressed funny. He ate differently from everyone else. I am sure people thought he was a little weird, but he didn't care. He was who he was because he knew what he was placed on this earth to do.

John had one purpose for his life–point to the coming of Christ. All four gospels reference the book of Isaiah and prophecy that was fulfilled through John the Baptist. Let's start there: *A voice of one calling: "In the wilderness prepare the way for the Lord; make straight in the desert a highway for our God"* (Isaiah 40:3, NIV).

This was John's purpose in life. He was the voice calling to say, "Christ is coming!" But how did he live with this purpose every single day?

First, John listened to God. In order to truly listen to God, John had to spend time with Him, and not just an occasional lunch, but a moment-by-moment journey with his Father. Scripture tells us John was in the wilderness. He was out there on his own listening to God. When God told him to start preaching, he went without hesitation. He was ready for the assignment God had before him.

Second, John knew who he was. He told the Pharisees he was not the Messiah, Elijah, or a prophet. He knew what he was created to do: to be the one who pointed to Jesus. John walked in this purpose, proclaiming the good news that was to come. He didn't talk about what he was doing (baptizing people into repentance), he told everyone who was to come: *"This is the one I meant when I said, 'A man who comes after me has surpassed me because he was before me." When he saw Jesus passing by, he said, "Look, the Lamb of God!"* (John 1:30, 36, NIV). Everything John did pointed to Jesus.

Today's world tells us to live our lives for ourselves and do everything we can to help ourselves. It feeds the lie that "it's all about me." John knew it wasn't about him; it was about Jesus. He lived his life pointing to Christ.

When you think about your own life, does it point to Christ or yourself? When you think of the things you have done, do you try to take the credit or do you say, "Look what Christ has done through me?"

> *And whatever you do or say, let it be as a representative of the Lord Jesus, and come with him into the presence of God the Father to give him your thanks.*
> Colossians 3:17, TLB

John gave us the ultimate example of how to point to Christ. Let's follow his example.

Dear Jesus,
Thank you for the example of John the Baptist. He knew who he was and what he was called to do. Help me see my identity in Christ and what He has called me to do. May everything I do in my life point to Him and lead others to want to know Him more. Amen.

<u>Scripture References</u>
John 1:19-36
Luke 3:1-18
Mark 1:1-8
Matthew 3:1-12

Reflection Questions

1. Do you spend time with God? Is it more of an occasional lunch, or do you seek Him moment by moment throughout your day? What does your time with God look like?

2. Where does your identity rest? Is it in who you are or what you're doing, or is it in Christ? What are four words God uses to describe you (your identity)?

3. Does your life point to Christ? Think of how you spend your day. Are you pointing to who Christ is in your life? Are you living in the purpose He has called you to?

Chapter 2
Respond to His Call

Today we are going to look at the disciples. These were the men that Jesus wanted around Him. He deliberately sought them out and called them to follow Him. Let's focus on how they responded.

In the Gospel of Matthew 4 and Mark 1, we see words like: *"At once they left their nets"* and *"Immediately they left their nets."* One translation even states, *"They didn't ask questions, but simply dropped their nets and followed."*

They were asked to follow Jesus and they went without questions. I don't know about you, but personally I would have a lot of questions: What should I pack? Do you know how long we will be gone? Where are we going? And, oh yeah, the most important–what are we gonna be doing?

The disciples didn't ask any questions. They immediately followed Him.

Then, as we look deeper into Luke 5, we see the disciples were out fishing but hadn't caught anything. They were tired and maybe a little frustrated, but here came Jesus. They were ready to go home and rest, yet He asked to preach from their boat. They said yes…but I wonder if they were reluctant. After He was done preaching, He told them to put their boats out to fish. They tried to explain to Him that they hadn't caught anything, but He still told them to cast out their nets. When they did, they caught more fish than their nets could hold. They caught so many fish that they had to have another boat come help them. When they got back on shore, Jesus said to them, *"I am going to make you fishers of men."* And they immediately left.

What?! They just left and followed Jesus. If that were me, I think I would have been celebrating all the fish I caught. I mean…ALL the nets were full. I probably would have turned to Jesus and said, "Can you give me a few days? I need to sell the fish. Make sure my family is all set. Finalize a few things. Then I will be able to follow you." But the disciples didn't hesitate. They immediately followed Jesus without question.

When I look at my own life, I have lots of questions that stand in the way of my following Jesus immediately. When I sense that He wants me to do something, I sometimes try to figure out how to fit it into my schedule. If I'm not careful, my calendar and my to-do list can drive my life. It can be so full that I don't have room to minister to someone when He tells me to.

Yet Jesus is calling me to be like the disciples. When He lays someone on my heart that needs help, He wants me to immediately respond with "I will help them." If a meal needs to be made or a task done, He doesn't want me to look at my schedule and see when I can prepare it. He wants me to step out and believe He will give me the time to make them something. When someone needs prayer, He wants me to immediately stop what I am doing and pray for them. These might seem like everyday ways we are following Jesus. They might seem small. But Jesus is trusting us with our small everyday yeses. Because when we are faithful with little, He will call us to be faithful with much.

Jesus is calling you and me to be like the disciples by immediately responding to what He is calling us to do. It is my hope and prayer that when we hear Jesus calling us to do something, we won't look at our schedules. We won't ask lots of questions. We will follow Him and be obedient to what He is calling us to do.

Dear Jesus,
I want to follow You whenever You call. Help me have the ears to hear what You are calling me to do. Help me to have the heart to want to do what You are calling me to do and the obedience to follow through with Your call. I don't want to live by my calendar and my to-do list. I want to live by Your timing and respond immediately to what You are calling me to do. Thank You for wanting to use me to reach others. My life is Yours. I am ready to respond immediately to You. Amen.

<u>Scripture References</u>
Matthew 4:18-22
Mark 1:16-20
Luke 5:1-11
Luke 16:10

<u>Reflection Questions</u>

1. Think about your life responsibilities, to-do list, and calendar. Do you let them drive your day?

2. What are three situations you have had in your life when Jesus was calling you to follow Him?

3. How did you respond to each of these situations?

Chapter 3
Stop the Noise

Have you ever noticed that there is a lot of noise in this world? Everywhere we go, there is noise. Car noise, radios, TVs, our children, people, our co-workers, our phones. It is never- ending, constant noise. Have you ever felt like you were drowning in the noise in your life? I know I have.

I wonder if Jesus ever felt this way. When He was on this earth, He was constantly surrounded by people and noise. He desired to minister to people, and the people wanted to hear His teaching and feel His healing touch. They were constantly around Him, asking Him questions and trying to be a part of his life. If that were me, I would have thrown my hands up in the air and screamed, "I've had enough!"

Not Jesus. He gave us a perfect example of what to do when we feel we are drowning from the noise: *"Yet the news about him spread all the more, so that crowds of people came to hear him and to be healed of their sicknesses. But Jesus often withdrew to lonely places and prayed"* (Luke 5:15-16, NIV). This isn't the only time we hear about Jesus withdrawing to a quiet place to just sit with His Father (Matthew 14:23, Mark 1:35, Mark 14:32, Luke 6:12). He chose to handle the noise in His life by spending time with His Father.

I love what Leah Di Pascal wrote in her First Five devotional, "When I Need to Get Away." She said, "Jesus loved the people He ministered to and had great compassion on them, but sometimes He chose to step away from the crowds. On a consistent basis, Jesus withdrew from people, daily life and the ongoing requests of ministry to find a place of peace and quiet. The location wasn't always the same, and the time of day would vary, but one thing was consistent. Jesus made a priority to set aside moments—sometimes hours or even all night long for silence, solitude and prayer." She goes on to challenge us to do this too. "Our ability and effectiveness as God's witnesses in this world is rooted first and foremost in our relationship with Him. And no matter how determined or strong we think we are, the constant demands of everyday life can eventually wear us down and deplete us. We need to be intentional and consistent in finding our own place of solitude. A quiet setting—away from all the noise and distractions—to pray and be aware of our heavenly Father's presence."[1]

For some of you, this is very difficult. You have children at home. You have their school work, your own job, and life in general. There is always noise, and the only time you get any quiet is when you lock the bathroom door. There might be some of you who have grown children like me, so you have more quiet and time. Yet you find when you sit down, there is so much noise in your head that you can't quiet your brain.

Jesus is calling us to go to this quiet place. He is waiting there for you. He wants you to rest with Him. I know when I do this, I am able to handle all the noise in my life. Whether you are someone who has a lot of noise from the outside world or a lot of noise in your own head, we all need to be intentional to seek that quiet place.

You may be asking yourself how to do this…first, you need to find that quiet place in your house, backyard, front porch, or even at your desk before the work day begins. Then, you need to find a time that works with your schedule. I am an early bird, so I like to seek Jesus first thing in the morning. I have a friend who is a night owl, so she seeks Jesus in the quiet of the night. You pick a time and place that works best for you, your schedule, and your personality. Jesus doesn't check the clock to see what time you seek Him. He just wants you to seek Him. And as you do, you will see that the noise in your life will not be so loud.

Dear Jesus,
There is so much noise in this world. I am sorry that at times I let it drown You out. Help me to find that quiet place, like You did, to sit with my Father. Help be intentional with creating this time daily. Even if it is only for a short time, I know that any time with You will refresh my soul. Thank You that You are always there to sit with me in the quiet. I look forward to our time together. Amen.

<u>Scripture Reference</u>
Luke 5:15-16

<u>Reflection Questions</u>

1. What type of noise do you have in your life? Is it from the outside world or in your head?

2. Where is a place that you can go and find some quiet in your life?

3. What is the best time of day for you to seek this quiet place?
Write out a plan to seek God this week.

Chapter 4
Respond to His Teachings

A little history about me, I was a teacher in special education and general education classes for twelve years. Though I haven't taught since 2019, I can still fall into my teacher role without even thinking because it's a part of me. I love helping people discover new things about the world around them and themselves. I believe that Jesus loved doing the same thing. Scripture tells us that Jesus was a teacher to ALL people He came in contact with. In Mark 10:1 (NIV), we see *"as was His custom, Jesus taught them."* In a different translation (NLT), we see *"as usual he taught them."* He never stopped teaching. Did you know that Jesus wants to be our teacher today? He does this through scripture, His letter to us. A good teacher will use different styles to help students understand what they are learning. That is what Jesus did. In scripture, we find Him teaching through storytelling, lectures, and asking and answering questions. We also see Him teaching in parables, simple stories used to illustrate a spiritual lesson. Whether we read one verse, a section, or a whole chapter, there's something in the Bible that Jesus wants to reveal to us.

If I'm not careful, I can get in the mindset of thinking that since I've already read a passage of Scripture before, I can read it again, but I'll just skim it. When I do this, I stop learning from the greatest Teacher there ever was.

I really wanted this year to be different and wanted to learn from Jesus again, so I asked Him, "Where do you want me to start? What do you want me to do?" I felt led to go to the book of Mark, and as I was reading, I noticed how the people responded to Jesus when He taught: *"The people were amazed at his teaching"* (Mark 1:23, NIV).

In Mark 1:29 (NIV) we see, *"news about Him spread quickly."* I believe the news spread quickly because they were so in awe of what He was teaching. They couldn't wait to share it with their friends.

My favorite is found in Mark 12:37 (NIV): *"The large crowd listened to him with delight."* They delighted in God's word as Jesus taught it. That is what I want. I want to open up His scripture and be amazed at His words and what He wants to teach me. I want to delight in what I am learning.

To delight in His Word, I need to be intentional with my time in scripture. I can't just read the words as quickly as possible, then go on with my day. I have to dive into what Jesus says, and I often do that by writing a verse I'm studying in my journal. Then I wait. What am I waiting for? For God to tell me what He is trying to teach me. He might highlight a word or phrase. Then I journal what I sense He is teaching me or asking me. I have journaled whole conversations with Him, sometimes even asking questions about what I am hearing. (Maybe I need to go back to chapter 2 and re-read about the disciples responding immediately.)

When a word jumps out at me, I enjoy looking it up in the original text (Hebrew or Greek) to see the intended meaning. I also love to read scripture in different translations. I never know which version is going to shout out what Jesus is trying to teach me.

The biggest change I have made when reading scripture is that I expect God to teach me.

"Incline your ear [to listen] and come to Me; Hear, so that your soul may live; And I will make an everlasting covenant with you, According to the faithful mercies [promised and] shown to David."
Isaiah 55:3, AMP

'Call to Me and I will answer you, and tell you [and even show you] great and mighty things, [things which have been confined and hidden], which you do not know and understand and cannot distinguish.'
Jeremiah 33:3, AMP

How can I not expect Jesus to teach me when I read these verses?

As I continue delighting in what Jesus is teaching me, I want everyone to know more about Him. He led me to start my Pause with God website (2Pausewithgod. com) in 2020. At 2PausewithGod.com , you will find opportunities to pause with Him through Quick Moments, video journeys (there are four of them), and my blog page. My heart is to encourage and inspire women to walk in the freedom and grace God has for them. I want to encourage women that even in the busyness of their lives they can take a moment 2 Pause with God.

Now the challenge is yours. Do you delight in God's word? Do you open up the Bible and expect Him to speak to you? If you do…PRAISE THE LORD! It's time to share with others. If you don't, it is time to start. Ask God to fill you with the excitement of reading His word, then hold on tight because the adventure is about to begin.

Dear Jesus,
Thank you so much that You have given me Your scripture to teach me what
You want me to learn. Lord, I pray that You would help me delight in your word
and be amazed at what I am reading. Whether I have read it for the first time or
the thousandth time, may I be in awe of the words You have for me. Give me a
teachable spirit to take what I am reading and use it for Your glory. Then help me
share what You are teaching me with others. I don't want to keep this to myself.
Thank you for being my teacher and always being with me. In Your name I pray.
Amen.

<u>Scripture References</u>
Mark 1:23, 28
Mark 6:2, 56
Mark 10:1
Mark 12:37
Isaiah 55:3
Jeremiah 33:3

<u>Reflection Questions</u>

1. When you open up scripture, do you expect God to teach you something, or are you just crossing it off of your list of things to do?

2. What is one way you can dig deeper into God's Word to see what He wants to teach you?

3. When God teaches you something, do you keep it to yourself or share it with others? Who can you share with today?

Chapter 5
Seek Jesus First

I am going to admit something to you...I am tired. It is not that there is anything seriously going on in my life. I am just tired of the worry that I allow to creep into my life. The anxiety. The stress. I have a talent for taking something really small, and working it over and over until it becomes a BIG worry. This makes me tired.

Jesus tells me exactly what I am supposed to do when I am worried and anxious–we find His solution in Matthew 6:25-34. He tells me not to worry. He says if God will take care of the birds of the air, how much more will he take care of me. And if God will clothe the flowers of the field in all their beauty and glory, how much more will he take care of my needs and clothes me. He even says that God knows exactly what I need, so don't worry about tomorrow.

Well, that is easier said than done for me. You see, I can be a master worrier, so how do I stop myself from spiraling into anxiety? Jesus tells me, *"Seek first his kingdom, and all these things will be given to you"* (Matthew 6:33, NIV). What does it mean to "seek Him first"? It means I need to make a conscious choice to not sit in the worry and anxiety in my life. I need to run to Him and His word. I need to run to Him in prayer and worship. When I do this, scripture tells me "all these things" will be given to me.

You may be wondering "what things"? What is He going to give me? When I seek Him first, He gives me peace (Philippians 4:7). He gives me assurance, joy, and strength (Isaiah 41:10). Not only does He give me things, He also takes things away like my worry, anxiety, and stress. He carries all of it on His shoulders. He is the peace that surpasses all understanding.

Here are some practical ways/techniques I use to help me seek Jesus first.
   • Find a short devotional that you can read in 5-10 minutes. There are so

many out there to choose from. Find one that brings you a sense of peace and joy.

- The Memory Bible App: Every time I find a verse that encourages me, I add it to this app on my phone. Then I can go back and look at it anytime. This is like the old days of writing verses on sticky notes, just more portable.

- Worship music list: I created a list on Spotify and Youtube of worship songs that lift me up when I am struggling. I will listen to a song (or songs) instead of sitting in worry.

- Go old school and write the verses on sticky notes or index cards. Then put them EVERYWHERE. In the kitchen, bathroom, on every mirror. In your car. Plaster your house with them.

Jesus says in Matthew 11:28 (NIV), *"Come to me all you who are weary and I will give you rest."* Jesus wants us to come to Him when we are anxious or worried. He wants us to seek Him first. When we do this, our days will be filled with his goodness. It is my prayer that when worry and anxiety try to overcome you, you will make a conscious choice to run to Him as you seek Him first.

Dear Jesus,
I admit that I can allow worry, stress, and anxiety to rule my life. But these are not from You. I want to run to You first when I am feeling overwhelmed with these things. You are my strength when I feel worried. You carry me when I feel anxious. Thank you that I do not go through any part of my day alone. Thank you that You want me to bring my burdens to You. Thank you that You are right there waiting for me to seek You first, and when I do, I receive joy, assurance, comfort, and a peace that surpasses all understanding. Amen.

<u>Scripture Reference</u>
Matthew 6:25-34
Matthew 6:33
Philippians 4:7
Isaiah 41:10
Matthew 11:28

<u>Reflection Questions</u>

1. What worries do you have in your life?

2. What barriers stand in the way of seeking Jesus first?

3. Write a prayer to Jesus, asking Him to move these barriers. Ask Him to help you make a conscious choice to always seek Him first. Ask Him for wisdom to show you what it means to seek Him first in your life.

Chapter 6
Faith the Size of a Mustard Seed

A few chapters ago, we looked at Jesus as a teacher and saw His heart to teach us through parables, stories, and examples. Today I want us to look at the parable of the mustard seed. We can find this parable in three of the Gospels: Matthew, Mark, and Luke. Then Jesus asked, *"What is the kingdom of God like? What shall I compare it to? It is like a mustard seed, which a man took and planted in his garden. It grew and became a tree, and the birds perched in its branches"* (Luke 13:18-19, NIV).

Jesus is talking about something that is very small. A mustard seed is only 1-2 millimeters in size, yet has the potential to yield a bush over 30 feet high and can nourish many birds and people. Jesus wants to do that with the faith we have inside of us. Faith the size of a mustard seed–something so tiny–can yield so much when given to Jesus. I love the examples in scripture of people who showed that small bit of faith when they were in trying circumstances.

Let's start with Jairus, the synagogue ruler whose daughter was very sick. He had faith that if Jesus would come to his house, his daughter would be healed: *"He pleaded earnestly with him, 'My little daughter is dying. Please come and put your hands on her so that she will be healed and live'"* (Mark 5:23, NIV). Jesus went with him, and after a brief delay (which we will look at next), arrived at his house, yet Jairus's daughter had died. The servants tried to stop Jesus, but He was on a mission. He commanded all the crying people to leave. *"Jesus took her hand and said "Talitha Koum!" (which means "Little girl, I say to you, get up"). Immediately the girl stood up and began to walk around (she was twelve years old). At this they were completely astonished"* (Mark 5:41-42, NIV). Jairus had faith that Jesus just touching her would bring healing, and IT DID!

Now let's look at the woman who had bleeding issues for years, which occurred right before Jesus healed Jairus's daughter. We don't even know her name, but we can learn so much from her. She had deep faith in what Jesus could do–she thought, *"If I just touch his clothes, I will be healed"* (Mark 5:28, NIV). She didn't even have to speak to Jesus. She didn't have to touch his physical body or have Him touch her–she believed that just touching His clothes would bring her healing, so she reached out and touched the hem of his garment. Jesus knew immediately that someone had touched him for healing. He told his disciples that someone had touched him, and they explained it away because of the crowd of people. But Jesus knew that someone had touched Him for healing. This woman came forward and explained that she KNEW if she just touched his cloak, she would be healed. Jesus responded to her, *"Daughter, your faith has healed you. Go in peace and be freed from your suffering"* (Mark 5:34, NIV).

I am going to get real with you. I have faith, but if I am not careful, I let worry creep in and stifle it. Right now, as I type this, I am spending more time worrying about a situation with my son than focusing on the fact that Jesus has already claimed victory over this situation. Jesus wants me to remember that I just need faith the size of a mustard seed for what He is going to do. I need to keep my eyes focused on Him and not the circumstances in my life.

What about you? Do you have something going on in your life that is weighing you down? Are you letting doubt and worry creep into your mind? Hold onto that little bit of faith that Jesus calls for, the mustard seed-size faith. Give it to Jesus because He wants to say to you, "daughter, your faith has healed you."

Dear Jesus,
I come before You now with all the struggles I have in my life. I acknowledge that I can be filled with worry and doubt. I am holding onto that mustard seed-size faith, because that is all I have right now, but You tell me it's enough. I am clinging to this promise and the promise of Your victory over all these struggles. In Your name I pray. Amen.

<u>Scripture References</u>
Matthew 13:31-32
Luke 13: 18-19
Mark 4:30-32
Matthew 9:18-26
Mark 5:22-43
Luke 8:40-55

<u>Reflection Questions</u>

1. What struggles do you have in your life? What is weighing on your mind and heart?

2. Do you trust Jesus to give you freedom from these struggles? Do you have the courage to touch the hem of His garment?

3. Write a prayer to Jesus sharing these issues, giving them over to Him. Admit to Him all the worry and doubt. Then give Him your mustard seed of faith as you trust Him to bring victory over these struggles.

Chapter 7
Faith Like a Child

In our last chapter, we looked at faith like a mustard seed. This week we are going to talk about having faith like a child.

People were bringing little children to Jesus for him to place his hands on them, but the disciples rebuked them. When Jesus saw this, he was indignant. He said to them, "Let the little children come to me, and do not hinder them, for the kingdom of God belongs to such as these. Truly I tell you, anyone who will not receive the kingdom of God like a little child will never enter it." And he took the children in his arms, placed his hands on them and blessed them.
Mark 10:13-16, NIV

As I thought about these verses, I wasn't sure what Jesus meant by telling His followers to approach Him with childlike simplicity. What does this look like? The more I meditated on this scripture, I realized that children trust unconditionally. They humble themselves before the adults in their lives. They listen (most of the time) and are dependent on the people around them. This is what Jesus wants from me. But how can I, as an adult, become like a little child?

People brought babies to Jesus, hoping he might touch them. When the disciples saw it, they shooed them off. Jesus called them back. "Let these children alone. Don't get between them and me. These children are the kingdom's pride and joy. Mark this: Unless you accept God's kingdom in the simplicity of a child, you'll never get in."
Luke 18:15-17, MSG

Jesus didn't want anything to get between the children and Himself. This made me stop and ask, what do I put between myself and Jesus? What was stopping me from coming to Jesus? Was it my pride? Maybe the thought that I want to control everything, doing it my own way? As a child, I was a handful, always trying to be in control. My parents loved me, offering guidance and direction to help me make wise choices. And when I listened to them, things often went better. This was what Jesus was doing with me. He was loving me, just like a parent, giving me the path to follow that will lead me in a direction that He desires.

When I reflect on this, I wonder why I would want to be in control of my life now? I know that when I try to control things, I am exhausted with no peace. I want to give up. Jesus wants me to give up my pride and humble myself before Him like a child. He longs for me to trust Him, living in dependency of Him as I walk through each day.

Jesus is asking the same thing to you, to give over your pride and need to control. He has victory over everything that is going to come before you. He is waiting with open arms for you to depend on Him. So climb into His lap. Be that little child who trusts in Him for everything.

Dear Jesus,
I acknowledge that I often have a need to be in control and independent. Help me remember that I can be dependent on You. That I can have that faith like a child. That I can crawl into Your lap and give everything over to You. As I walk through today and every day to come, help me give everything over to You as I trust in Your perfect plan. In your name I pray. Amen

<u>Scripture References</u>
Mark 10:13-16
Luke 18:15-17
Matthew 19:13-15

<u>Reflection Questions</u>

1. What do you put between yourself and Jesus (pride, need to control, independence, etc.)?

2. Write a prayer to Jesus laying these things at His feet. In this prayer, climb into His lap and surrender all to Him.

Chapter 8
Let's Nibble on God's Word

I have always been fascinated by the Martha and Mary story. I like to make lists and get tasks done, and I love crossing things off my list as I finish them. I am a Martha. Recently I was reflecting back over time with my husband's family when we were first married. Our families were very different. His family was very spontaneous, and my family was more time oriented and task oriented. I remember getting frustrated when we would make dinner plans and things wouldn't happen at the time we had said. I would be waiting and many of them were often downstairs playing music. I now see that in my frustration I missed something very important – the relationship. I missed the time of just being together as a family. From there, I started thinking about my time of serving in the church. As a Martha, I love to serve. I often serve wherever needed because that is what He told me to do. Suddenly I found myself asking the question, "in my service am I missing something? Am I so busy doing that I am missing the relationships He has planned for me." I started questioning why I was serving? In my uncertainty, God led me back to the story of Martha and Mary.

You remember Martha and Mary in the Gospel of Luke. The sisters who loved Jesus. As we look back on their story, we see that Jesus was staying with them. Martha was scurrying around trying to get things done because she wanted everything to be extra special. Mary, however, was sitting at Jesus' feet. Martha wasn't happy, and approached Jesus and said, "Lord, tell her to help me." And He responded, "Mary has chosen what is best."

This story really bothered me. I wasn't sure I liked Jesus' response. Is there something wrong with me being a Martha? I have the gift of hospitality and I want everyone to feel welcome in my home. Instead of stewing over my frustration, I went to one of my Bibles. I am so thankful for the extra note that I found in The Quest Bible that asks, "What was wrong with Martha's hospitality?": *Nothing, however, her priorities were out of order. She was so concerned with the task of serving, that she missed the task of greater importance to sit at Jesus' feet. Life's greatest priority should be to take in and reflect on what God would have us do."* [2]

Lightbulb moment!!!   I was missing out on a relationship with Jesus because I was so busy serving Him. That is not what Jesus wants. He is more interested in our relationship with Him than how we are serving Him, so my question became, what did I need to do to cultivate my relationship with Him?

Taste and see that the Lord is good.
Psalm 34:8, NIV

Like Mary, I have discovered that God's word is nourishment to me. The sweet taste of reading God's word and taking it in is the nourishment I need throughout the day. Just like I eat three meals a day, I need to get into His word many times during the day. I need to nibble on God's word as often as I can and in many formats. It is through time in His word that I strengthen my relationship with Him. I am still a Martha, serving Him where He calls me throughout the day, but I have found that my service for Him is so much sweeter because of the time I am spending with Him.

Some of the ways I have developed to get into His word are: devotional reading first thing in the morning, listening to a podcast at lunch, listening to Christian music throughout the day, working on my study from my church Life Group, and reading a book by an author I enjoy. When I am doing these things on a daily basis, I am working on the sweetest relationship I could ever have–a relationship with Jesus, my Lord.

What about you? Are you so wrapped up in serving that you miss the relationship Jesus wants to have with you? Take a moment in the afternoon or early evening to take a sweet nibble at God's word. Taste and see how good He is.

Dear Jesus,
Thank you for Your word that guides me. Thank you that You have given it to me as a love letter from You to nourish my soul. Help me to find ways to get into Your word throughout my day. Not because I have to, but because I want to. I want my relationship with You to be the most important thing in my life. Thank you for meeting with me whenever I read Your Word. In your name I pray. Amen.

<u>Scripture References</u>
Luke 10:38-42
Psalm 34:8

<u>Reflection Questions</u>

1. Reflect on the story of Mary and Martha. Which one are you?

2. Do you take time in your day to spend in the Word? Is it just once, or are you seeking Him out throughout your day?

3. What ways are you seeking to get into God's word? What new ways do you want to add to your life?

Chapter 9
Learning to Worship

Today we are going to talk about worship. Have you thought about what worship is to you? When I first came to know Christ, I thought worship was getting together on Sunday mornings.   As I grew in my walk with the Lord, my view of worship changed. Worship also became the quiet time I spent with Him in scripture, prayer time, listening to music, and fellowship with other believers. I am so thankful for the sanctification process and Jesus growing me in my understanding of worship. Jesus tells us exactly what worship is supposed to be when He talks to the Samaritan woman in the book of John.

It's who you are and the way you live that count before God. Your worship must engage your spirit in the pursuit of truth. That's the kind of people the Father is out looking for: those who are simply and honestly themselves before him in their worship. God is sheer being itself—Spirit. Those who worship him must do it out of their very being, their spirits, their true selves, in adoration.
John 4:23-24, MSG

Worship is everything that is inside me–everything I am. It has to come from my heart and my true being. I really like what Matthew Henry said in his Bible commentary on John 4:23-24: "we must worship him with fixedness of thought and a flame of affection, with all that is within us." [3]

In my journey to learn more about what worship is, I was led to a short article on the website Worship Team Coach, "The 5 Greatest Expressions of Worship in the Bible."[4] My eyes were opened to the deeper meaning of worship through the points of the article:

<u>Praise God no matter your circumstances:</u> Paul and Silas were men who sang praises to God after they were beaten and put in prison (Acts 16: 2226). "When

we are faced with trials and hardships, let's remember that Satan may buffet our bodies but he can't imprison our praise!"[5]

It is easy to praise God when things are going well. But do I praise Him when I am in prison? Recently I have been sitting in the prison of uncertainty for the future. My son has been in school to be a chiropractor, taking after his dad. He is now uncertain if this is what he is supposed to be doing. He has taken a break from chiropractic college and is waiting to hear from God, which leaves the future of our office uncertain. The plan had been he would join us, and Dad (and I) would slowly phase out, leaving the business to him. Now we don't know what is going to happen. I don't like uncertainty. The plan we had in place is on hold, or even null and void. But what should I do? Praise God! I know He is making a way with the perfect plan. So rather than sit in my uncertainty, I am choosing to PRAISE GOD!

<u>Surrender everything to the will of God:</u> Jesus surrendered His will by going to the cross to fulfill God's plan (Luke 22:41-43). Quote from the article: "On the evening of his arrest, Jesus prayed for another option, if possible, than the cross. But then, he uttered the most amazing worship statement ever known when he said, "Not my will, but yours"."[6]

I need to surrender my will of what our future is going to look like. Retiring in a few years, downsizing our house, and buying a camper has always been my plan. I have dreamed of us camping in every state in the continental USA. Will any of this happen? I don't know. But God does. Through this season, He is teaching me (and Chris) to trust in Him for what our retirement will look like. He has also been teaching me to surrender what my plans are for my boys. He has something amazing planned, and I need to step out of the way.

<u>Be obedient to God:</u> Abraham was willing to sacrifice his son, Isaac because God told him to (Genesis 22:12-14). Quote from the article: "Obedience, in the eyes of God, is even greater than any sacrifice or gift we could give Him. In obedience, we will reach new heights in our worship experiences. "[7]

God has been hitting me between the eyes with saying YES to Him, which is one of the reasons you are reading this devotion. I said yes to Him to rework a video journey I had done during Covid into a written devotion. Right now I am doing my best to say yes to Him by sitting and being still in His presence. No planning or organizing, just spending time with God. If you need help learning to say yes,

I highly recommend you read *I'll Say Yes* By Amber Olafsson. God used it to speak to me about saying yes to Him in the little things.

<u>Praise God no matter how you are viewed by others:</u> The woman with the alabaster jar was an outcast. She was not someone of importance, yet she gave everything she had in spite of what people thought of her (Luke 7:36-50). Quote from the article: "In one moment, she pressed through fear, prejudices, shame, and created one of the most intimate moments of worship in the Bible."[8]

Getting real again . . . I am struggling with the fact that my son is struggling about what his tomorrow is supposed to be. You see, all of his friends are graduating from college and starting their next adventure. He is now very uncertain what this next adventure is for him. My heart wants to be happy for all of his friends and their moms who are bragging on Facebook, but our story is different and a bit sad. This woman didn't worry about anything except worshipping Jesus with what she had: her alabaster jar, her tears, and her heart.

<u>Give all that you have:</u> The widow gave all that she had. She didn't compare herself to what others gave. She gave from her heart (Mark 12:41-44). Quote from the article: "What moved this woman to give everything she had to God remains a mystery, but what is clear is that God considers our giving an act of worship. People will judge the size of our God by the cost of our worship. If we can stop holding so tightly to our money and possessions, and allow the Christ-like character trait of generosity to manifest in our lives, we may discover a deeper worship encounter than we've ever known."[9]

Convicted! Yup . . . that is me. I am so good at the comparison game in how I serve or what I give to God. Let's not even talk about the earthly comparison trap I can fall into. This widow taught me that I need to give from my heart. Not so others will see, but so God will be glorified.

Jesus calls me to worship him inside my very being, with everything that I am, and with everything I do. Guess what . . . He is calling you to worship Him in the same way. Will you join me?

Dear Jesus,
You have opened my eyes to what worship truly is. I pray that You would help me worship You with all I am. Help me learn to say yes to You in the little things. I desire to put You first with my time and talents. I ask You to show me what this looks like. I want to praise You even when life is difficult and I don't know what

to do next. I trust what You do and that You are working. I want to surrender everything to You so I can follow Your plan for my life. In Your name I pray. Amen

<u>Scripture Reference</u>
John 4:23-24
Acts 16:22-26
Luke 22:41-43
Genesis 22:12-14
Luke 7:36-50
Mark 12:41-44

<u>Reflection Questions</u>
1. How do you describe worship?

2. Reflect on the 5 ways of worship above. Is there one that is easier for you? Harder?

3. Write a prayer to Jesus to help you walk in worship with Him.

Chapter 10
Surviving the Storms in Life

The weather is unpredictable. Some days are beautiful and sunny, then suddenly it all changes. Thunderstorms, rain, or frigid temperatures pop up out of nowhere. I find that I just roll with whatever the meteorologist predicts the weather will be. I grab a jacket, maybe some gloves, an umbrella, or even my sunglasses and head into my day. But what do I do when the storms come up in my life?

Recently I've had many storms hit me all at once. A financial storm. An emotional storm. A medical storm. I found out that I didn't roll with them as easily as I do the changes in the weather, unless you count rolling to the refrigerator.

Jesus taught me exactly what I am to do when there are storms in my life. In Luke 8: 22-25, we see the disciples and Jesus were out in a boat when a storm came up. The disciples became very fearful. They looked back and saw Jesus sleeping. They couldn't believe it. They woke Him up and asked, "Master, how can you be sleeping? Surely we are going to die?" Jesus said to them, "Where is your faith?" Jesus could definitely ask me this same question with the storms I have been experiencing. Where is my faith? Am I spending more time worrying about the storms than I trusting Jesus? (I better go back and read chapter five again!)

In Matthew 14:22-31, Jesus told me exactly what to do with the storms in my life. Again, the disciples were out in a boat. Jesus was on the shore and he started walking to them on water. They were very afraid. They thought he was a ghost. Jesus said, "No, it is me." Peter replied, "Lord, if it is you, let me walk on water towards you." Jesus told him, "Come." So Peter got out of the boat and started walking towards Jesus. Because he had his eyes on Jesus he was able to walk on the water. But when he looked around and saw the water and wind, he became very fearful and started to sink. Peter took his eyes off the one thing that could help him in the midst of the storm. He took his eyes off of Jesus.

How many times do I take my eyes off Jesus when a storm arises? Do I look at my bank account and worry about how I am going to pay that next bill? How many times have I searched the internet when the doctor says I want to order a test? I can't even count the number of times I have turned my eyes to the refrigerator when I am emotionally struggling.

This is not what Jesus wants. He wants us to fix our eyes on him when we are in the storms of our lives. We know we can trust Him. Jesus is the light that shines in the storm. The storm might not end right away. It might be weeks or years. But no matter what, we need to keep our eyes on Jesus, the faithful light in the storm. How do I do this? By spending time with Him daily. By reading His word. By seeking Him in prayer. By listening to Christian music. By sharing with other believers my struggles and asking for prayer. All these things help me keep my eyes fixed on Him. I also need to remember, *"What is impossible with man is possible with God"* (Luke 18:27, NIV).

Dear Jesus,
I don't like the storms that are in my life. I admit I don't always respond as I should when a storm arises. Help me keep my eyes fixed on You no matter what the storm is. Help me not worry about how the wind is raging around me, but to trust in the protection You are providing. I know this storm is only for a season. I trust Your perfect timing to bring me out of this storm, and I will give You all the glory for making it to the other side. Amen.

<u>Scripture References</u>
Luke 8:22-25
Matt 14:22-33

<u>Reflection Questions</u>

1. What storms have you experienced in your life?

2. What things do you turn to when in a storm?

3. Identify three ways to personally fix your eyes on Jesus during the storms of your life.

Chapter 11
When Bigger Isn't Better

We recently experienced the spring time change where clocks were moved
forward an hour. So what used to be 4:00 am was now 5:00 am. Boy, was it dark
out when I woke up Monday morning, but I turned on some lights and started
my day. The light was bright, and I could do what I needed to do. Jesus tells us in
Matthew 5: 14 - 16 (NIV) what he wants us to do with the light he has put in each
one of us, *"You are the light of the world. A town built on a hill cannot be hidden.
Neither do people light a lamp and put it under a bowl. Instead they put it on its
stand, and it gives light to everyone in the house. In the same way, let your light
shine before others, that they may see your good deeds and glorify your Father in
heaven."*

I remember when I first read this verse I thought, "I am going to do something
great and mighty for God! I am going to let His light shine!" I waited to see
what that big thing was going to be. And I waited...and I waited. I realized I
didn't know what great and mighty thing God wanted me to do. How could I
let His light shine if He didn't show me the BIG thing He wanted me to do for
Him. Then I started thinking about the different people He put in my life and
how they let His light shine through them. I realized it wasn't through big and
mighty things, but through the little things they did. It was through the friends
who walked beside me when I was discouraged and needed support. It was
the community of friends that surrounded me when I went on bed rest with my
youngest son. For two months, people brought us meals, did our laundry, drove
our older son to school, played with our two year old, and even cleaned my house.
One young man really wanted to help us during this time. He was single and not
a good cook, so he brought us Kentucky Fried Chicken for dinner. You see, he
heard I had been craving KFC and wanted to bless me. This little thing (and all
the others) spoke so much to me and my family. This was the light and body of

Christ in action.   It wasn't one person but many people responding to the little thing God called them to do. I saw the Light of the Lord shine brightly as each person added their little spark.

What about you? Do you have someone in your life that has shown you Christ's light? Someone who did something small, but it meant the world to you? In today's busy world, it is easy to miss these little things. Take a moment and think about the little things that helped you in your time of need.

Maybe you are like me, waiting to see what that BIG thing is that God wants you to do. Stop waiting and start looking for the little things you can do for those around you. They are there. All you have to do is say yes.

I want to challenge each of you to start noticing the little things people are doing for you. Take the time to thank them and let you know you see them, then look around you and see who you can be the light of Christ to. Think of something that may seem little to you, but will be BIG to them and Christ. It is time for you to be the city on the hill shining brightly for Christ.

Dear Jesus,
You are the light of the world and You live inside me. I don't want to spend my days looking for the big way You want me to shine your light. Help me see the little things You want me to do. Help me be faithful in these little things to those around me. Thank You for all the people You have put in my life that shined Your light to me through the little things. Together we are a city on a hill as we shine Your light to others. Amen.

<u>Scripture References</u>
Matt 5:14-16

<u>Reflection Questions</u>

1. Who are people that shine brightly for Christ in your life? What did they do?

2. Who is someone (or many someones) that you can shine Christ's light to? What can you do to shine his light? Remember it doesn't have to be big.

Chapter 12
Jesus . . . Where Are You?

Today we are going to explore the parable of the lost son in Luke 15. Do you remember the story? There were two brothers. The younger son went to his father and asked for his inheritance. The father gave it to him. He took it, striking out on his own, and spending it on whatever he wanted. He was destitute. He took a job working with pigs. One day, he realized that these pigs are eating better than he was and that if he just went home, things would be better. He decided to go home and ask for his father's forgiveness.

Now his father has been waiting for him to return. When he sees him in the distance, he runs to him. He was so excited that his son had returned home. He brought out his best robe and put it on him. He throws a party for him with his best food. He celebrated that his lost son had come home.

Now let's look at the older son. When he returned from the field, he saw this big party. He wondered what was going on. He was told that his brother had returned and that his father was throwing a big party. Instead of being happy that his brother had returned home, he was filled with irritation and anger. He never went anywhere, always working beside his father. Yet his father never threw a party for him. This brother refused to go to the party. He became bitter and angry at all that his father was doing for his little brother. His father went searching for Him and all he could do was complain, "why haven't you done this for me and my friends?"

Wow, this is just like the soap operas my grandma used to watch. Both of these sons had issues that caused family drama. The younger son was selfish, with no self-control. The older son was angry, bitter and complaining. Both of these sons were separated from their father because of their own actions. Yet, their father was always right there...hopeful and waiting.

When I first started my walk with Jesus, I thought I had to be one son or the other. Now, after many years of walking with Him, I realized that I have been both sons during different seasons in my life.

There have been moments when I was selfish, thinking only of myself. I remember a day when I was working at a long term care facility as the recreational therapist. We had documentation we needed to complete on each of our residents. There was one binder that held the paperwork we needed to complete for the week. All of the therapists would need to use this same binder. I was having a horrible day and still needed to complete the documentation. I walked into the office thinking I would be out of there in no time. Of course, every other therapist had the same thought, and they got there before I did. I was so frustrated, I slammed my binder down, grumbled under my breath, and stormed out of the room. Not one of my finer moments and certainly not how God wanted me to be a witness for Him. I was only thinking of myself and the fact that I wanted to go home. Not only did my boss talk to me, but Jesus convicted me of how I responded. Like the younger brother, I realized I was thinking only of myself. The next day I apologized to all the ladies I worked with.

I am embarrassed to admit that there have probably been more times when I was angry, bitter, or complaining. Most of the time it is because I have been comparing my life to others. They seemed to be getting the party while I am sitting outside getting nothing. I get in these moods when I spend too much time on Facebook. I've had many pity parties when I see all the extravagant trips people have taken. The jealousy monster rears its ugly head and I become upset. Older son syndrome at its finest. Complaining to God that He hasn't given me more. I will discount all the wonderful trips I have taken because they don't live up to what other people are doing.

Whether I was the first or second son, I was only thinking of myself and what I wanted. I wasn't close to my Heavenly Father because I was too busy looking at my own wants. My attitude was "it is all about me," which separated me from God. Not because of anything He did, but because of what I was doing.

Both sons give us examples of how they handled their attitude. The older son remained bitter and angry, but the younger son acknowledged his mistake. Scripture says he realized he was separated from the goodness of his life with his father. He returned to him and asked for forgiveness.

What about you? Which son do you resonate with? Are you being selfish, doing your own thing, or are you bitter and complaining? Maybe you are like me, having moments when you are them depending on the day? Let's follow the example of the younger brother. Let's return to our Heavenly Father who is waiting with open arms.

Dear Jesus,
I know that you are always there for me. I know I can become selfish and want to do my own thing. When I do, help me run back to your open arms. I know I can get irritated and think that life isn't fair. When I do this I become bitter and turn away from You. Help me lay my frustrations and bitterness at Your feet. I want to see all that You have done for me and be thankful. May my eyes always be on You. In Your name I pray. Amen.

<u>Scripture References</u>
Luke 15

<u>Reflection Questions</u>
1. Which son do you relate to the most? The younger son or the older son?

2. Do you see the Father standing there waiting for you? If not, what is standing in the way of you seeing Him?

3. Write a prayer to your Heavenly Father asking him to forgive you for whatever has separated you from Him. He is waiting for you with open arms.

Chapter 13
Let's Celebrate Jesus

Over the last twelve chapters, we have taken a look at Jesus' life and His ministry
on Earth. Today we are going to look at His Triumphal Entrance into Jerusalem.
Most of us celebrate this day as Palm Sunday. The people were so excited
that He was coming to town and believed He was going to change the world.
While Jesus was on this earth, He performed many miracles of healing, calmed
the storms, and fed thousands of people a number of times–even the demons
listened to him. He stood up for the outcast and the poor. They believed that He
was their deliverer! I have a note in my bible that says, "They believed He was
their political messiah to lead them to independence from the Roman Empire." [10]
Whether they realized who He really was or what His plan was, they were excited
that He came to town. The people celebrated Jesus as they would celebrate a
victor returning from battle or a King returning home by waving palm branches,
which were often used during times of celebration. Jesus was in the center of the
procession, and the people all around him were shouting, *"Praise God for the Son
of David! Blessings on the one who comes in the name of the Lord! Praise God in
highest heaven!"* (Matthew 21:9, NLT). They saw victory coming.

I am going to get real with you. I mean, we have been together a long time now.
We are sisters, and sisters get REAL with each other. How would I respond
if Jesus were to come to my hometown today? Would I be outside looking
for Him? Would I be waving my hands in the air or waving palm branches to
celebrate Jesus coming to town? Would I be in awe that He was coming to my
town and want to celebrate all that He had done? Or would I be so wrapped up in
my own struggles and circumstances that I miss seeing Him.

So here is the real part . . . I hate it, but my heart is so heavy with circumstances
that I am missing my opportunity to celebrate who Jesus is. I am so uncertain of
the future that I forget Jesus came to earth to secure my future. I am embarrassed

to tell you that this past weekend was Easter, and I didn't celebrate Jesus as I should have. My heart, mind, and soul were wrapped up in my circumstances. Ouch! That is so hard to admit to myself and to you. But it is the truth.

I love how Eugene Peterson translated 1 Peter 4 in The Message, *Friends, when life gets really difficult, don't jump to the conclusion that God isn't on the job. Instead, be glad that you are in the very thick of what Christ experienced. This is a spiritual refining process, with glory just around the corner* (1 Peter 4:12-13, MSG).

Talk about conviction. I can't believe I am thinking God isn't on the job and isn't working. I know He is,but I don't feel it right now. It is taking too long. So as I sit here reading this verse, not once or twice, but over and over and over again…it is like a deep breath to me.

Inhale God, exhale my circumstances.

Inhale Truth, exhale lies.

Inhale peace, exhale stress.

God is refining me and my family as we walk this road. His glory is right around the corner in my circumstances,which is something to celebrate. Even in the midst of my struggles, God is moving!

> *We know that all things work together for the good of those who love God, who are called according to his purpose.*
> Romans 8:25, CSB

I am going to choose to celebrate who Jesus is! Celebrate Him as the people of Jerusalem did.   Celebrate all He has done in my life and my family's lives over the years! I know I have been called for His purpose. I know my circumstances are in His hands, and He is going to use it for His good and glory. How do I know this? Because *Jesus Christ is the same yesterday, today, and forever* (Hebrews 13:8, CSB). When I rest in this, I can do nothing but celebrate Jesus!!!

Dear Jesus,
I am so sorry that I have let the circumstances of my life cause me to take my eyes off of You. I know You are moving in my life, and You have everything figured out. I am claiming the victory You have for me (and my family). Today I am

choosing to celebrate who You are! I am choosing to celebrate all You have done in my life in the past! I am choosing to celebrate all You are doing through the circumstances in my life. I am choosing to celebrate YOU! In Your name I pray. Amen

<u>Scripture References</u>
Matthew 21:1-11
Mark 11: 1-11
Luke 19:29-44
John 12:12-19
1 Peter 4: 12-13
Romans 8:25
Hebrews 13:8

<u>Reflection Questions</u>
1. Do you have circumstances in your life that are stopping you from celebrating who Jesus is? Take a moment to confess these circumstances to Jesus.

2. What are ways you can celebrate Jesus during these difficult times?

3. Reflect on your life and all those times that Jesus saw you through the tough times. Take a moment to celebrate what He did for you during these times.

Chapter 14
My Role in the Crucifixion

Don't you just hate emotional rollercoasters. One minute you're celebrating life and everything is good, then the next minute something happens, and discouragement and frustration set in. Last chapter we were celebrating who Jesus was as He entered Jerusalem, yet after this wonderful show of love and celebration, Jesus is arrested. The people who celebrated Him at the beginning of the week are now yelling for Him to be crucified. Pilate, who doesn't think that Jesus should be crucified, tried to convince them that Jesus needed to be set free. No matter what he said, the crowd continued to yell, "crucify Jesus!" Pilate gave into the crowd and Jesus was sentenced to death.

As I was reflecting about all of this, I found myself asking the question, "Did anyone stand up for Jesus?" We see in scripture that the disciples scattered when Jesus was arrested. We read in Luke that Peter disowned Him three times. Peter was one of the inner circle of friends to Jesus, and they had a special relationship. Yet Peter still disowned Him.

Then Jesus was crucified. We call it Good Friday, but this day seems anything but good. Jesus was nailed to the cross. He died. He was buried. When most people look at it, they see darkness and sadness. The sky goes dark, the veil is torn. Jesus was placed in a tomb. His death seems so final. Is this the end? NO! It doesn't stop at the tomb . . . because we know the rest of the story. Which we will continue with in the next chapter.

But before we move on, we need to acknowledge our role in Jesus' crucifixion. What would I have done if I was there? Would I have stayed by His side or would I have scattered like the disciples? What do I do today? Am I like Peter? Do I disown Christ with my silence? Do I speak up for Him with my friends and family? Do I speak up for Him in my community? What about Facebook? If people were to friend me on Facebook, would they see that I defend Jesus? How many times have I been afraid to speak up for Jesus thinking I would offend someone? Am I like those people in the crowd, celebrating Him one minute and crucifying Him the next?

These are questions each of us need to ask ourselves. We need to examine our hearts to see where we stand with Jesus. Are we by His side defending Him to the world, or have we deserted Him like the disciples? We need to admit to ourselves where we stand. Because when we do, we are ready to truly embrace the rest of the story.

Dear Jesus,
I don't want to be like the people in Jerusalem. I want to be the person that defends You to the world. Search my heart, Lord, and show me when I have deserted You. I know I have not stood up for You as I should. Convict me of these times and change my heart for the future. Help me to be bold for You! In Your Name I pray.
Amen

<u>Scripture References</u>
Matthew 26:69-75
Matthew 27:15-25
Mark 14:66-72
Mark 15:6-15
Luke 22:54-62
Luke 23:13-25
John 18:15-18
John 18:38-40

<u>Reflection Questions</u>

1. Reflect over your Journey with Jesus. Can you name a time (or two) when you stood up for Jesus to someone else?

2. Can you name a time (or two) when you didn't stand up for Jesus to someone else?

3. Write a prayer to Jesus…thank Him for the times you have been bold and repent of the times you have been silent. Ask Jesus to give you the strength and courage to always be bold for Him.

Chapter 15
Victory!

How can this chapter be titled victory? In our last chapter, we discussed Jesus' death. He was crucified on a cross and placed in a tomb. Where is the victory in that? Ohh . . . keep reading . . . the victory is there!

Jesus' body had not been prepared for burial because of Passover, so when Passover ended, the women who loved Him went to prepare His body. When they got there, they saw the stone had been rolled away and Jesus was not inside. Two angels came to them and said, *"Why do you look for the living among the dead? He is not here; he has risen! Remember how he told you, while he was still with you in Galilee: 'The Son of Man must be delivered over to the hands of sinners, be crucified and on the third day be raised again.'" Then they remembered his words* (Luke 24:5b-8). Jesus talked about the temple being destroyed and built up again in three days. Everyone thought He was talking about an earthly building, but He wasn't. He was talking about Himself (John 2: 19-21).

The women went back and told the disciples that Jesus' body was missing. They weren't sure what to believe, and some of them were very afraid. Jesus met them in their fear and showed them He had risen. Thomas was not among them, so he didn't believe what everyone was saying.

Now Thomas (also known as Didymus), one of the Twelve, was not with the disciples when Jesus came. So the other disciples told him, "We have seen the Lord!" But he said to them, "Unless I see the nail marks in his hands and put my finger where the nails were, and put my hand into his side, I will not believe." A week later his disciples were in the house again, and Thomas was with them. Though the doors were locked, Jesus came and stood among them and said, "Peace be with you!" Then he said to Thomas, "Put your finger here; see my

hands. Reach out your hand and put it into my side. Stop doubting and believe."
Thomas said to him, "My Lord and my God!" Then Jesus told him, "Because
you have seen me, you have believed; blessed are those who have not seen and yet
have believed."
John 20:24-29

Jesus appeared to Thomas and met Him right where he was, in his doubt and
uncertainty about His resurrection.

What about you? Who do you think Jesus is? Do you think that this is just a
wonderful story to read? Maybe you think Jesus is just a prophet or somebody
special who lived on this earth. Or do you see Him as the Son of Man who went
to the cross for you? Have you ever thought, why did Jesus do all of this, why
did He go to the cross? Or maybe you're thinking, what does this have to do with
me? Maybe you don't understand the victory. Keep reading . . . this is when it
gets really good!

God loves you. He wants a relationship with you. But he can't because of the sin
in your life. Now you might think you don't sin that much, or when you do, it is
not that bad. I mean for the most part you're a good person. You treat people well
and help whenever you can. Yet, our God is perfect and He can't look at our sin,
even if it is just one.

God loves us so much that he sent Jesus to this earth. You see, Jesus was fully
man, but never sinned. Jesus was sent to be a sacrifice for us.

For God made Christ, who never sinned, to be the offering for our sin, so that we
could be made right with God through Christ.
2 Corinthians 5:21, NLT

When Jesus went to the cross, He took all our sin on Him: *Surely he took up our*
pain and bore our suffering, yet we considered him punished by God, stricken
by him, and afflicted. But he was pierced for our transgressions, he was crushed
for our iniquities; the punishment that brought us peace was on him, and by his
wounds we are healed. We all, like sheep, have gone astray, each of us has turned
to our own way; and the Lord has laid on him the iniquity of us all (Isaiah 53:4-6,
NIV).

When Jesus died on the cross, the veil in the temple was torn: *And [at once] the*
veil [of the Holy of Holies] of the temple was torn in two from top to bottom; the

earth shook and the rocks were split apart (Matthew 27:51, AMP). This veil was there to separate us from God because we were not worthy to be in His presence. I love the footnote on BibleGatway.com for this verse: *"God tearing the veil of the Holy of Holies is significant in that it symbolizes that God's presence was now open to all people and not just the High Priest."*[11]

God's presence is open to you! All you have to do is trust what Christ did on the cross! Trust that He died for you and did this because He loves you. Christ wants to have a relationship with you. He has removed your sin by His death and is seated at the right hand of the Father.

Who then is the one who condemns? No one. Christ Jesus who died— more than that, who was raised to life—is at the right hand of God and is also interceding for us.
Romans 8:34, NIV

When I read this verse, I see Jesus leaning over to God saying, "You see this one. She knows me. She trusts me. I paid the debt for her sins. She is a part of our family!"

See…that is the victory! Jesus conquered death! He is seated at the right hand of the Father and He is the reason God can look at you. Jesus' death sealed your relationship with God. God no longer sees your sins. That's the victory we are celebrating! And as we celebrate, we see that the journey has just begun!

Dear Jesus,
Thank you for the victory you offer me. A victory that allows me to walk in relationship with You. Today I want to celebrate that victory! Today I want to live the life of victor. I want to live a life as the daughter of The King! I am ready…let the journey begin! In your name I pray. Amen

<u>Scripture References</u>
Luke 24:1-8
John 2: 19-21
John 20:24-29
2 Corinthians 5:21
Isaiah 53:4-6
Matthew 27:51
Romans 8:34

<u>Reflection Questions</u>

1. Who do you think Jesus is? A man? A Prophet? The Son of God? The Savior of the world?

2. Can you identify a specific day when you put your trust in Jesus as your savior? Reflect on your life. Do you journey with Jesus every day, once a week, or every so often?

3. Write a prayer to Jesus acknowledging who He is in your life. Thank Him for the victory He gave you.

Next Steps

You may be thinking that your journey is over now that you have reached the end of this devotion. No . . . **YOUR** journey is just beginning. The question you need to ask yourself is what are you going to do with it? In order to do that, you need to get real with yourself. Look back over your reflection questions from chapter 15. How did you respond? Below are different sections. Pick the one that best describes your relationship with Jesus. This is where your journey will begin.

<u>Not sure you have a relationship with Jesus</u>

Can you specifically identify a day when you put your trust in Jesus as your savior? If not, then today is your day! A day where you start your journey with Him by your side. Reread chapter 15 to remind you of the victory Jesus offers you. If you are ready to ask Jesus to be your savior, pray the following prayer:

Dear Jesus,
I thank you for this devotion that You put in my hands. Thank you for opening my eyes to how much I need You. I know that no matter how hard I try, I will sin. I want a personal relationship with You, but my sin stands in the way. I trust in your death on the cross as a payment from my sins. I trust in Your resurrection which offers me a life with You. A life to walk in the freedom You have for me. I invite You to be the Lord of my heart and my life. In Your name I pray. Amen

Welcome my dear sister! You are now a daughter of the King. He has some amazing plans for you as you journey with Him.

> *"For I know the plans I have for you," declares the Lord, "plans to prosper you and not to harm you, plans to give you hope and a future."*
> Jeremiah 29:11, NIV

Check out the next steps to help you on this journey.

<u>Have a relationship with Jesus, but not living as you know He wants you to</u>

Maybe you are someone who has always known Jesus as your Lord and Savior, but you haven't been living for Him like you should. This was the case with one of my boys. He grew up in our Christian home. He watched his dad and me walk with Jesus. He accepted Christ as a boy and participated in all the church activities. But when he got into high school, he started to live for himself. He knew that Jesus had died for his sin, he just wasn't living the life Jesus had planned for him. I am so thankful to a pastor who shared Matthew 7:21-23 with him. God used this verse to help my son want to live his life moment by moment for Christ.

"Knowing the correct password—saying 'Master, Master,' for instance—isn't going to get you anywhere with me. What is required is serious obedience—doing what my Father wills. I can see it now—at the Final Judgment thousands strutting up to me and saying, 'Master, we preached the Message, we bashed the demons, our super-spiritual projects had everyone talking.' And do you know what I am going to say? 'You missed the boat. All you did was use me to make yourselves important. You don't impress me one bit. You're out of here.'"
Matthew 7:21-23, MSG

This isn't what God wants for you. He wants to welcome you with open arms and say well done good and faithful servant (Matthew 25:21). Today is the day that you can renew your commitment to Jesus. Let this prayer be the prayer of your heart.

Dear Jesus,
I confess that I have not been living for You. Forgive me for all the times I have chosen to follow my own plan. I want to change and live for You. I ask You to fill me with the Holy Spirit so that I may see You clearly. Help me to surrender my desires and walk with You every moment of every day. In Your name I pray. Amen.

I am so excited for you! God has such amazing plans for you. You are His masterpiece designed for a purpose. Hold on tight my sister, your journey with Him is about to get exciting!

<u>Have strong relations with Jesus</u>

There is nothing better than walking moment by moment with Jesus. But I don't need to tell you that. You're there! What I want to do is thank you and encourage you. You are a light to the world around you. You may not see all that you are doing, but God does. He sees you are in His word and in prayer for others all the time. He delights in you. Keep it up my friend! The following prayer is my prayer for you as you continue your journey with Christ.

Dear Jesus,
Thank You for the lady reading these words. A lady who is walking with You and shining You to the world around her. I ask that You would give her a sense of Your presence and strength today. I ask that You would fill her with Your spirit so that she may do more than she can even ask or imagine. I know You have her right where she is. That she was created for a time such as this. That You have an amazing calling on her life. Give her the courage and strength to step into this calling You have for her. May she remember, she never walks alone, for You are always with her. I can't wait to hug her when we all get to heaven. In Your name I pray. Amen.

Next Steps for EVERYONE
It is time to get excited! Your journey with Jesus will never be the same.

There are a few things all journeys need: ***planning, preparation, and prayer.***

Plan how you are going to spend time with Jesus. What works best for you in this season of your life. Go to your calendar and block off time with Jesus. Remember, you don't have to schedule an hour block. Jesus is happy with any amount of time. Find 5 minutes every hour if that is all you can do. Those 5 minutes add up to a whole lot of time with Jesus. Think it isn't possible or won't do much? I beg to differ with you. This devotion book was written in little bits and chunks while I was working. You see, I am at our office 10-11 hours a day. God has taught me how to take every little chunk of free time and give it to Him. You will be surprised at how He will take your few minutes with Him and multiply it for His good and glory.

Prepare how you will spend time with Jesus. There are so many resources out there to spend time with Jesus: devotionals, bible studies, books on specific topics, fiction books, blogs, podcasts, TV shows, music, and the list goes on. Find something that works for you. Ask friends what they like to read. Look for a bible study to join. Join a Christian book club. If you can't find anything local, look online. That is what I did. I am part of the *Armor Up Women: Kingdom Warriors* growing in the Word group on Facebook. This group of ladies from all over the world have helped me grow in my knowledge and wisdom of what it means to walk with Jesus.

Pray for God's guidance on where He wants you and what He wants you to read. Over the years, I have watched Him lead me to just the right group of ladies, at just the right time, doing just the right study. If you can't find a local bible study, I challenge you to start one. That is what I did twenty-nine years ago. I wanted to study God's word with other women. I couldn't find one…so I started one. Your walk with God will increase in ways you can't even imagine when you offer to facilitate a group for Him. If you need help knowing how to do this, I am here for you! Check out my resource page for ways to contact me.

Still not sure where to begin. Check out my video *"Journey to Transformation"* on my website (see my resource page). This is my journey of "Walking with Christ, to be more like Christ, till I am face to face with Christ". Who knows… this might even be my next book.

It is hard for me to close out this journey with you. I find myself getting a little tearful as I write these last paragraphs. I want to thank you for journeying with me to the Cross. It is my prayer that you have grown closer to Jesus as we walked this road together. There is a saying, "God wants to write your story, stop trying to steal the pen." For so many years I was writing the story and inviting God to join me. Not anymore. When I totally surrendered that pen to Him, my journey truly began. Ladies, it is your turn. Surrender the pen and get ready to walk in the purpose and plan He has for your life.

Additional Notes

1. DiPascal, Leah. "When I Need to Get Away". FirstFive.org. Proverbs 31 Ministry. NOvember 24, 2016. app.first5.org/book/Luke/ff_luke_9

2. What was wrong with Martha's Hospitality?, "Luke" in The Quest Study Bible (Zondervan Publishing House, Page 1437)

3. Henry, Matthew. "Matthew Henry's Commentary – Verses 4–26." BibleGateway. HarperCollins Christian Publishing, Inc.https://www.biblegateway.com/resources/matthew-henry/John.4.4-John.4.26

4. Guest Writer. Worship Teamcoach. https://www.worshipteamcoach.com/biblical-worship/the-5-greatest-expressions-of-worship-in-the-bible/

5. Ibid

6. Ibid

7. Ibid

8. Ibid

9. Ibid

10. Why put coats and branches on the roadway, "Mark" in The Quest Study Bible (Zondervan Publishing House, Page 1399)

11. Matthew 27:51 (AMP). Bible Gateway. HarperCollins Christian Publishing, Inc, https://www.biblegateway.com/passage/?search=Matthew%2027%3A51&version=AMP

 Shannon is a woman who knows what it means to be busy. A perfectionist at heart, she can be so busy she misses the intimate walk with God. She desires that all women learn to take quick moments to Pause with God in the midst of their busy lives. What started as a Facebook page to encourage friends (November 2020) has grown into the 2 Pause With God ministry. Shannon has shared her personal journey to the cross as she beat the busyness in her own life to draw closer to Christ. She is part of the leadership team at her church and a life group/bible study facilitator. Shannon has shared her personal journey as a speaker at Women's events in her area and facilitated a breakout session at The Light Conference.

Shannon has been married to Chris for 25 years. She is mother of four boys, two beautiful daughter-in-loves, and a grandmother of six. Camping has become a great way for Shannon, Chris, and their dog Maggie to unplug from the busyness. They are proud to be Ultimate Outsiders in South Carolina by visiting all the State Parks and Historical Sites. She also enjoys cooking, reading and watching movies. When not ministering at church or exploring state parks, Shannon works with Chris in their chiropractic office. This is a family run business that allows them to minister to their community through chiropractic care.

Let's Connect

My heart is to encourage and inspire women to walk in the freedom and grace God has for them as they take time out of their busy schedules 2 Pause with God.

Website
https://www.2pausewithgod.com/
Video Journeys / Blog pages / Quick moments

Email
2PausewithGod@gmail.com

Join me on Facebook:
facebook.com/PausewithGod

9 781952 840913